For my grandson Philip K.L.
To Madeleine Edmondson J.C.

Editor: Wendy Boase
Art Editor: David Bennett

THIS IS A BORZOI BOOK PUBLISHED BY ALFRED A. KNOPF, INC.

Text copyright © 1985 by Alfred A. Knopf, Inc.
Illustrations copyright © 1985 by Kenneth Lilly
Copyright © 1985 by Walker Books Ltd.
All rights reserved under International and Pan-American
Copyright Conventions. Published in the United States by
Alfred A. Knopf, Inc., New York. Originally published
in England by Walker Books Ltd, London.
Distributed by Random House, Inc., New York.
Manufactured in Italy 10 9 8 7 6 5 4 3 2

Library of Congress Cataloging in Publication Data
Cole, Joanna. Large as life daytime animals.
Summary: Brief text and life-size illustrations present
the characteristics of a variety of small animals.
Includes the ermine, squirrel monkey, bee hummingbird, birdwing
butterfly, and others.   1. Animals – Juvenile literature.   [1. Animals]
I. Lilly, Kenneth, ill.   II. Title.
QL49.C673   1985   599   85-4301
ISBN 0-394-87188-X   ISBN 0-394-97188-4 (lib. bdg.)

LARGE AS LIFE
Daytime Animals
LIFE SIZE

Paintings by Kenneth Lilly

TEXT BY JOANNA COLE

ALFRED A. KNOPF · New York

Little Blue Penguin

The smallest penguins in the world never see ice and snow. Little blue penguins live on the beaches of Australia, not at the South Pole like most other penguins.

These babies would fit easily in your two hands. But they wouldn't want to stay there. They are waddling down to the water for a swimming lesson.

Red Squirrel

This red squirrel is getting ready to jump.
It spreads its legs far apart and leaps from
one tree to another. Its bushy tail comes
in handy for balancing.

When the squirrel sleeps, it uses its tail
another way. It wraps the tail around
itself like a warm blanket.

Queen Alexandra's Birdwing Butterfly

Live birdwing butterflies are exactly the same size as this painting of them! The female birdwing is the largest butterfly you'll ever see.

The male is smaller than the female. You can see him standing on a spiky red flower. He is tasting it at the same time. Butterflies taste with their feet, not with their tongues!

Lesser Spotted Woodpecker

Why does a woodpecker tap-tap-tap on a tree? It is looking for food. From the sound, the woodpecker can tell if an insect is hidden under the bark. Then it bores a hole and gets the insect out with its long tongue.

Woodpeckers make a larger hole in a tree for their nest.

Common Tree Frog

Most frogs live in ponds. Tree frogs are the only ones that live up high. Sticky pads on their fingers and toes help them climb trees. Their tongues are sticky too, and they use them to catch insects like the ladybug.

When it rains, the tree frog climbs under a leaf to keep dry.

Eastern Chipmunk

Chipmunks don't wear clothes, but they do have pockets. Inside each cheek is a roomy pouch for nuts and seeds. One small chipmunk can carry seventeen nuts at once!

Black-tailed Prairie Dog

These roly-poly animals aren't dogs. They are a kind of squirrel. They are called prairie dogs because they live on the American prairies and "talk" to each other with barking sounds.

When this prairie dog family hears a warning bark, they will all dive into their burrows until the danger is past.

Bee Hummingbird

Its fast-beating wings make it hum like a bee. It sips nectar from flowers like a bee. But it is not a bee. It is the smallest bird in the world.

The bee hummingbird weighs less than half a teaspoon of sugar. Its nest is the size of a thimble. In fact, the bee hummingbird is so small it has to be careful not to get caught in a spider's web!

Ermine

The ermine doesn't seem to be hiding, but it is. Its white fur blends in with the snow. The ermine makes its living by hunting mice and other small animals. Camouflage – blending in – helps it sneak up on its prey.

When summer comes, the ermine changes its color and its name. Its coat turns brown and people call it a stoat.

Squirrel Monkey

Is there a yellow monkey almost as small as a banana? Yes, a squirrel monkey. This mother squirrel monkey would fit inside your school bag. And her baby could go in your pocket.

The monkeys' yellowish green color matches the trees where they live in the rain forests of South America.

Nature Notes

Red Squirrel
(Sciurus vulgaris)

The red squirrel is nimble, busy, agile, and completely at home in the trees. It jumps with ease, can cling to the smoothest bark, and always hurtles head-first down tree trunks. Sometimes it hangs by its clawed hind feet, its thick tail giving it balance. A squirrel's tail can measure 8 inches, almost as long as its whole body. Different kinds of red squirrels live in woods, parks, and bushy fields in Europe, North America, and Japan. They come to the ground only to find food and to bury nuts and acorns for the winter. Hazelnuts are favorites. Red squirrels do not hibernate, but in very cold weather they huddle together in nests, wrapping their tails around themselves for warmth.

Little Blue Penguin
(Eudyptula minor)

Steering with its tail and feet and using its wings as paddles, the little blue penguin is as quick and agile in water as a fish. But penguins are birds, although they cannot fly. Unlike most penguins, however, the little blue lives in warm waters and on sandy beaches, sometimes walking over a mile inland to lay its eggs. The world's smallest penguin, it is found on the southern coasts of Australia and New Zealand and islands nearby. For a flightless bird generally less than 16 inches tall, life on the beach is dangerous. Both the penguin and its eggs are at the mercy of cats, dogs, foxes, rats, ferrets, snakes, and gulls. Chicks, if they survive, are eight or nine weeks old before they learn to swim. Then life is much safer!

Queen Alexandra's Birdwing Butterfly
(Ornithoptera alexandrae)

In the rain forests of Papua New Guinea the chenille plant, with its spikes of small red flowers, is one of many plants that provide food for birdwing butterflies. A butterfly sips nectar from flowers with its long coiled tongue, called a proboscis. The biggest and heaviest butterfly in the world is the female Queen Alexandra. She weighs over 3½ ounces and has a wingspan of up to 12 inches. The male is much smaller but makes up for this with brilliant colors. Birdwings fly with slow rhythmic wing - beats and short glides, usually high in the treetops. Few birds or insects bother them because their bold colors and patterns show that they don't taste good. They have more to fear from butterfly collectors.

Common Tree Frog
(Hyla arborea)

Tree frogs like to sit on stems and sun themselves, but if they get too hot or the weather changes, they jump nimbly underneath the leaves. These tiny frogs, only 2 inches in length, are very skillful acrobats. With their long hind legs they can jump and catch insects in midair; their webbed feet help them to make parachute-style landings; the adhesive pads on their fingers and toes allow them to cling to the slenderest branches. The common tree frog lives in marshes, reedy banks, damp meadows, and gardens in most of Europe and some parts of Asia. In spring the females lay about 1,000 tiny eggs at a time, in clumps the size of walnuts. The tadpoles, when they hatch, are less than ¼ inch long!

Lesser Spotted Woodpecker
(Dendrocopus minor)

This woodpecker is just 5½ inches long, but it drums and drills with the energy of birds twice its size. It taps trees in search of grubs, beetles, and caterpillars to eat. It also eats fruit and seeds. The red-capped male drums rapidly to proclaim his territory or to attract a mate. With their long pointed beaks, both male and female drill and gouge out their nest-hole high up in a branch. Like all woodpeckers, the lesser spotted is a good climber, using its stiff tail as a prop. It hardly ever perches or lands on the ground. Shock - absorbent tissue between its beak and skull prevents the bird from getting severe headaches. Its rat-a-tat-tat can be heard in orchards, parks, and open woodland all over Europe, in England, and in parts of Asia and North Africa.

Black-tailed Prairie Dog
(Cynomys ludovicianus)

This animal is a burrowing squirrel and not a dog at all. It is named for its doglike yelp, as well as for the color of its tail. Prairie dogs live in underground colonies on the plains of North America. The basic group is the family, of perhaps ten animals, who eat, sleep, and play together. Each family digs its own set of tunnels, with several entrances or exits. Above ground, sentries watch constantly for danger. The prairie dog, 12 inches long and weighing only 2 pounds, has many enemies: snakes, eagles, hawks, coyotes, ferrets – and farmers, who destroy it because it eats their crops. In winter, when snow covers the ground, prairie dogs curl up and hibernate until spring.

Eastern Chipmunk
(Tamias striatus)

Chipmunks are frisky, inquisitive animals, but very cautious. At the first sign of danger, they scamper for their burrows. The chipmunk is a kind of squirrel that lives underground. This type of chipmunk is found in forests in eastern parts of North America. When they excavate their burrows, chipmunks are careful to hide their activity. They carry the earth away in their cheek pouches and scatter it in the bushes. These cheek pouches can also hold an astonishing amount of food. As winter approaches, chipmunks collect nuts, acorns, and seeds. In the far north they sleep right through winter in a state of hibernation. Chipmunks can be tamed and make lively pets. For an animal about 10 inches from head to tail, even a watering can is a home big enough for two!

Bee Hummingbird
(Mellisuga helenae)

The bee hummingbird's tiny wings beat so rapidly that only a blur and a bee-like hum tell you that it has wings at all!
Bee hummingbirds can fly backward, forward, up, down, or sideways at great speed. They loop and roll and dive as expertly as stunt pilots. They even drink and bathe in flight by skimming over wet leaves. These birds spend most of their day hovering at flowers such as the hibiscus, sucking up the sweet nectar that gives them energy. They have beautiful iridescent feathers that glitter and flash in the sunlight, but the male, with his red head, is more brilliant than the female. Both birds are under 2 inches long. The bee hummingbird lives in woodlands, shrubberies, and gardens in Cuba.

Squirrel Monkey
(Saimiri sciureus)

Squirrel monkeys are inquisitive, active, noisy, quarrelsome, and extremely agile. In the rain forests of South and Central America, they live and travel in groups of up to 100, leaping swiftly through the trees in single file as if playing follow-the-leader. They use their tails for balance when jumping and for support if they stop to rest. The tail is longer than the whole body, which is less than 12 inches in length. Squirrel monkeys spend nearly all their time in trees, catching insects, tree frogs, and snails; stealing birds' eggs; and snatching berries, nuts, and fruit to eat. They are easily tamed and, with their appealing features and acrobatic talents, are popular pets. The biggest pet squirrel monkeys ride easily on the backs of the local dogs!

Ermine
(Mustela erminea)

Ermine is the name given to a stoat when it has shed its brown summer coat and grown a winter one, which is usually pure white except for the black tip of the tail. Perfectly camouflaged against the snow, the ermine hunts rabbits, hares, mice, voles, small birds, fish, and reptiles. Although it is less than 18 inches long including its tail, the ermine is a very fierce hunter. But because it hunts gamebirds and domestic poultry, farmers lay traps for it. It is also killed for its snowy fur. Ermines live in many wild places, as well as near farms, in the British Isles, Europe, North America, and northern Asia. Ermines are alert, energetic, and immensely curious animals, leaping, tumbling, and wrestling in play, and often standing up on their hind legs when hunting.